Private Gardens of Connecticut

Jane Garmey ✤ Photographs by John M. Hall

THE MONACELLI PRESS

For Stephen Garmey and Mary McConnell

Published in the United States by The Monacelli Press, a division of Random House, Inc.
1745 Broadway, New York, New York 10019

The Monacelli Press and M design are trademarks of Random House, Inc.

Library of Congress Cataloging-in-Publication Data

Garmey, Jane.
  Private gardens of Connecticut / Jane Garmey ; photographs by John M. Hall.
    p. cm.
  ISBN 978-1-58093-241-7
  1. Gardens--Connecticut. 2. Gardens--Connecticut--Pictorial works. I. Hall, John M. II. Title.
  SB451.34.C8G37 2010
  712'.609746--dc22
                      2010016520

Printed in China
10 9 8 7 6 5 4 3 2 1
First edition

Designed by Susan Evans, Design per se, Inc.

www.monacellipress.com

The Gardens

Introduction

FIRST, A CONFESSION. I am addicted to gardens. I love being in my own, but
I also get enormous pleasure from going to other people's, talking to them, smelling
their roses, and listening to their plans. It's a pleasure I didn't know I was missing
until I caught the gardening bug. That happened in the 1970s when my husband
and I became the owners of a dilapidated eighteenth-century saltbox in northwest
Connecticut. It came with a lot of untended grass and little else in the way of land-
scaping. Since my husband was preoccupied with the structure of the house, it
seemed logical that the out-of-doors should be my responsibility.

Knowing almost nothing about even the most basic principles of horticulture, I was
hardly a willing recruit. I am English and grew up in England and, to my astonishment,
I found my American friends assumed that the English are born with a grasp of the
subtleties of successful composting, know how to prune, and could, of course, tell the
difference between a rugosa rose and a hybrid tea. My pleas of ignorance were inter-
preted as false modesty and there was general disbelief when I tried to explain that
neither of my parents were the least bit interested in anything to do with gardens.
The only formative experience in horticulture I can remember was going with one
of my aunts—a passionate rosarian—on a trip to Whipsnade Zoo to collect buckets
of elephant dung with which to cover her roses.

But back to my garden. It suffered not only from my lack of experience but also from
the rigors of Connecticut's harsh winters and sweltering summers, and even the occasional hurricane. While my neighbors took these conditions in stride, my English
friends were incredulous when I told them of dawn raids by hungry deer, surprise incur-
sions by egg-laying snapping turtles, temperatures that dropped well below minus ten
degrees in the winter, snow in April, and once even frost during the last week of May.
But, somehow as I began to learn some of the complexities of gardening in a country
with ten different hardiness zones, I got hooked and soon there was nothing I liked
better than going to see gardens and learning from their owners how to work around
the limitations of this unforgiving climate. So, when many years later the chance
arose to do a book with my friend, photographer John Hall, about private gardens of
Connecticut, I couldn't believe my good fortune.

Connecticut is the third smallest state in America (ninety-five miles by sixty-five miles
at its widest point), but its topography is surprisingly varied, stretching from the shore-
line of Long Island Sound to the Litchfield Hills and from the suburbs of New York
to well north of Hartford. Home of patriot Nathan Hale, actress Katharine Hepburn,
writer Mark Twain, and composer Charles Ives, Connecticut is known for its insurance

industry and its state flower (mountain laurel) but not particularly for its gardens, in spite of a rich garden history.

Toward the end of the nineteenth century, Greenwich emerged as a fashionable sub-urb of New York, and Connecticut's coastline began to attract a succession of summer visitors, including New Yorkers with power and money such as William Rockefeller (John D.'s brother), Lewis Lapham, one of the founders of Texaco Oil Company, and Edmund Converse, the inventor and founder of U.S. Steel. These industrialists created vast estates with palatial European-inspired gardens, or chose American landscape architects such as Frederick Law Olmsted, Charles Gillette, Fletcher Steele, Warren Manning, Beatrix Farrand, and Ellen Biddle Shipman to design their gardens. The gardens of one estate in Greenwich were so vast that more than fifteen gardeners were required to maintain them. Morton Plant's Branford House near Groton boasted an astonishing sunken water garden with a circular fountain and mounded beds designed by landscape architect Guy Lowell. Eolia, the elegant summer mansion of the Harkness family, set on over 230 seaside acres of sweeping lawns at Goshen Point, a little south of New London, started out as an Italianate garden with colonnaded loggias but was later redesigned by Beatrix Farrand in the style of an English Edwardian garden.

Sadly, most of these gardens have not survived, and many of the grand ones were turned into tennis courts or swimming pools in the 1950s. One of Beatrix Farrand's gardens was replaced with sod in order to make an outdoor seating area, while that of Standard Oil heiress Annie Burr Jennings ended up as a residential subdivision. Others literally went to seed after years of neglect as the expense of maintaining their labor-intensive outdoor rooms became too great. There are some exceptions, the two most notable being Eolia, now Harkness State Park, and Hill-Stead House in Farmington, both of which are open to the public today and give a sense of what that grand and lost tradi-tion was all about.

For this book, we were not, however, searching so much for historical gardens as for twentieth-century work. Inevitably, we have seen more gardens than we could possibly include and inevitably there will be those who disagree with the choices we have made. But, here, another confession is in order. This book was never intended to be a compre-hensive survey of private gardens in Connecticut, but is instead a personal and often idiosyncratic selection. Our criteria were simple. We wanted to include gardens from as many parts of the state as possible and to focus on the wide diversity of styles from formal to small, contemporary, wild, and old-fashioned. Some of those we selected had never been professionally photographed while others had been published, and in some cases frequently. Some are open to visitors a few times a year through the Garden

Conservancy's popular Open Day Program; others do not participate. Some are grand in scale, others exceedingly modest but all have been cared for with great love. None of these gardens was made overnight and many have taken years to come to fruition. The garden of the Greek god Adonis may have "one day blossomed and fruitful were the next" but not any of the gardens featured in this book.

As I crisscrossed the state searching out gardens, I was struck again and again by how essentially rural Connecticut still is. Even Hartford, its capital and second largest city with a population of 124,512, is tiny by today's standards. In spite of its small size, Connecticut's climate is tremendously variable, incorporating three different plant hardiness zones. Its landscape too is surprisingly varied, encompassing 618 miles of magnificent coastline, untold acres of glorious open farmland, and steep wooded hills. The one connecting thread to be found in every part of the state is, however, stone.

Connecticut once had hundreds of quarries, although not many survive today. The stone from each was unique, a testament to the state's complex geology. Granite from Stony Creek in eastern Connecticut became the base of the Statue of Liberty and was used in building New York's Grand Central Terminal, while rich chocolate-colored sandstone from Portland, near Middletown, was the most common building material of the nineteenth century and gave its name to many thousands of New York town-houses. Today, what we most notice are the miles and miles of long winding iconic stone walls that traverse the state and are a poignant reminder of Connecticut farming. In the seventeenth and eighteenth centuries these dry stone walls were stacked and laid without the aid of any concrete mortar. Made to fence in animals, divide farming pastures, and delineate property lines, they were strictly utilitarian. Today they are one of the most distinctive features of the Connecticut landscape, their lyrical lines testimony to their mostly anonymous builders. Every garden in this book makes use of local stone in one way or another, be it for walls, pathways, or extending rock ledges, and whether intentionally or by happenstance, stone is incorporated into their overall design.

Writing tends to be a solitary occupation so I feel extremely lucky to have had the opportunity to collaborate with a remarkably talented photographer. Seeing a garden through John's eyes, discussing what makes it unique, and deciding how and what to focus on has been an eye-opening experience. In writing about gardens, the seventeenth-century poet Andrew Marvell refers to their "delicious solitude." That description holds true for all of the gardens in this book. They are personal and private in the best sense of the word, and to make each of them come alive to others, the camera must capture the garden's personality and the text reveal it. I hope that we have succeeded.

A Connoisseur's Creation

Like many good gardeners, Anne Bass rarely leaves the house without a pair of clippers in hand. For her, deadheading and pruning are not mundane tasks but one of the essential pleasures of garden life. Experienced, knowledgeable, and passionate about her garden, which she began in 1999, she has created a series of beautiful outdoor spaces that are carefully linked to make a compelling whole. Bass understands the virtue of restraint, and her garden is the more memorable for its structure and simplicity.

Rock Cobble Farm lies in a valley that was once three separate farms, and the various houses and barns on the property have been meticulously restored as have its indigenous dry stone walls. The resulting landscape of hills and valleys, extending as far as the eye can see and bound by a network of perfectly preserved low stone walls, forms a startlingly beautiful outside perimeter to the garden that Bass has created immediately around her own house, a reconstructed barn brought from Pennsylvania. This inner cultivated garden includes a rose garden, medicinal herb garden, a terrace garden filled with hydrangeas, a high-walled cutting garden, a magnolia walk, and an extensive woodland garden.

Few would argue that for sheer drama the rose garden takes the prize, and it is at its most spectacular from mid-June to mid-July, when the color, scent, and sheer abundance of buds and blooms is overwhelming. The design of this rectangular space is extremely simple: grass paths intersect five beds that are neatly edged in boxwood and laid out in parallel lines. A high hornbeam hedge and a row of *hydrangea Paniculata* growing behind a stone wall frame the garden on two sides and a wooden pergola, interplanted with clematis and climbing roses, runs across the end of the rose garden that is furthest from the house.

Bass uses no herbicides, although she once admitted that she might bend this rule were it necessary to save a single rose. That remark, spoken in jest and not intended seriously, reveals her intense devotion to the more than 140 varieties of roses that she has collected. Russell Page, the celebrated landscape designer who worked many years ago on her garden in Fort Worth, Texas, and became her friend and mentor, believed that different types of roses should be planted together so should one fail, there would be no empty space while trying to find a replacement. She has followed this advice, using color as her organizing principle. Within this astonishing mix of hybrid, floribunda, shrub, and musk roses, the palette shifts almost imperceptibly from blue to red to purple. Mauves lead to pinks, and soft pink to apricot and white. Thanks to Page's influence (he insisted she write out her plant orders in Latin) Bass not only learned the Latin names for plants but also acquired the discipline of keeping meticulous records. Her "master list" includes the name and classification of every rose and also gives its source,

color, and approximate height, as well as referencing alphabetically the bed in which it can be found. This kind of precise attention to detail is just one indication of how serious Bass is about every aspect and detail of her garden.

Since Page had died by the time Bass purchased her farm, she asked Dan Kiley to lay out a terrace and devise a plan for the overall layout of the garden around the main house. It was very much a collaboration and while she respected his ideas, they did not

always agree. She loved his proposal for a terrace that would have an indented wall of dry stone, a miniature bosque of plane trees, and pots of hydrangeas and jasmine, but when he wanted to cut down a row of magnificent maples in the adjoining field and replace them with larches, she declined. His thought was to have a ha-ha divide the garden from its surrounding farmland; Bass preferred traditional dry stone walls and she prevailed. They agreed on a three-sided avenue of pleached linden trees to connect the house to the swimming pool but when Kiley proposed a holly hedge to enclose the rose garden, she opted for hornbeam. He suggested a steep grass slope in the medicinal herb garden. However, Bass foresaw problems with the mowing and steered him toward terracing.

Later, Madison Cox helped with some of the detailed planning for the medicinal herb garden, a classically simple garden that is close to the house and has the spirit and feel of a French medieval cloister. A series of simple criss-crossed box-edged parterre beds, planted with nepeta, calamintha, and old-fashioned dianthus and punctuated at each corner with freestanding balls of boxwood, lead to a small round pond, formerly an old cider press found in the English Cotswolds, at the center of the garden's axis. Huge showy lotus flowers float ethereally above the water and a low stone wall frames the natural landscape that lies beyond. Two rows of six square-shaped beds in front of the wall are each planted with a different herb. The selection may change from year to year but in the past has included artemisia, lavender, rosemary, mint, rue, lemon verbena, and basil.

The cutting garden, enclosed by a ten-foot wall of hornbeam, was begun in 2002. A cedar pergola, thickly covered with grapes and clematis, runs its full length and

blackberries have been trained to grow up its three arched entrances. There are neatly pruned espaliers and cordons of apples and pears. The paths between the beds are grass and the beds, edged with low boxwood and a single row of Belgian blocks, are planted with fruit and flowers. Blueberries, gooseberries, red and white currants, fraise de bois, and strawberries cheerfully cohabit with dahlias, peonies, iris, Japanese anemones, baptisia, and sweet peas. Giant alliums provide early summer drama, and Meyer lemon trees in pots, brought out from the greenhouse later in the season, add to the luxuriance of this potager.

The woodland garden was the unexpected result of a decision to build a tennis court. Hearing of someone who had placed a court at such a distance from their house that to reach it required a considerable walk, Bass decided to site hers on top of a hill beyond the woods at the far end of her cutting garden. This gave her the opportunity to create a woodland garden. Still in its early days, it is planted with shade-loving plants such as hellebores, epimedium, species peonies, trillium, ferns, and thousands of spring bulbs. Rare shrubs and specimen trees continue to be added. One of Bass's most recent finds is a rare variegated *Kousa*, a species that she once saw in Normandy.

Bass views her garden as a work in progress, providing opportunities and challenges at every turn. Although no one can predict what direction her future landscape may take, given the style, discipline, and restraint of what she has already accomplished, one is inclined to suspect that, as Russell Page once wrote, "it can scarcely take another form than one which is a true reflection of its maker."

22

Echoes of Le Nôtre

A third of an acre within view of the New Canaan train station is the site of the remarkable achievement of Richard and Sandra Bergmann (she generously insists he is the eye and she is the weeder), who have brilliantly transformed what was a rather ordinary space into a formal, geometric garden that is playful, original, and highly architectural.

Bergmann is an architect by profession, who later became interested in landscape design and is now also a registered landscape architect. It was thirty-six years ago that he and his wife bought their 1836 Greek revival townhouse, which had once belonged to the distinguished editor Maxwell Perkins. Wanting to make a garden in the narrow space around the house, they first did their research and then set off to France with Michael Kenna's book on the great seventeenth-century French landscape designer André Le Nôtre as their guide. Next, they took a trip to Charleston, famous for its side-yard gardens, and then another to England to look at more gardens. They also studied the philosophy of Chinese gardens, where spaces are made through building rather than planting. This concept became Bergmann's inspiration as he set out to make his own garden, using greenery, gravel, stone paving, Belgian block, and wood as his building materials.

His intention was to make a small garden appear larger through the use of steps and terracing. "I am very interested in the way one moves through outdoor space," he says, going on to explain, "I don't want people to see the garden all at once, but only in turns and bends, in bits and pieces." And the garden he has designed is indeed full of surprise. From a small parking area at the side of the house, visitors walk past a row of six upright clipped European beech trees. Rounding the corner, directly in front of the house, they come face to face with the green geometry of a dramatic silhouette of cone- and pyramid-shaped yews. "These are a play on the huge yew cones that became Le Nôtre's signature style in so many of his gardens," says Bergmann, "but it was only after looking at English gardens and seeing how much the English love garden follies that I realized I could take these cone shapes, reduce them to a miniature size, and squeeze them in together, thus creating my own garden folly."

But go past the Le Nôtre moment and on to the small parterre garden, made entirely of clipped yew. Turn the corner and see how a gentle slope of no particular consequence has been transformed into a gravel garden running the full length of one side of the house. A series of shallow steps edged in Belgian block terrace the space nearest the house, descending to frame two shallow circular fountains. A diagonal line of Belgian block cuts across the space to play with the perspective. There is a hemlock grove, planted by Maxwell Perkins's wife in 1934, along the edge of the property,

which offers privacy and protection from the neighboring house, its canopy providing the backdrop for a small seating area. Ignoring advice that it was too shady for anything to grow there, the Bergmanns underplanted the hemlocks with a mix of ferns—Japanese painted, Lady, Victorian, Ostrich, Goldie's, New York, and Wood—to make a small woodland garden. Thanks to a drip irrigation system, the ferns are very much alive and well.

Beyond the steps on the topmost level of the terrace are four clipped *Malus* 'Adams' crab apples set in raised square planters made of stained pressurized wood (ideal for sitting on) and underplanted with creeping Jenny. To accentuate their presence in a shady corner of the garden and to make them "pop out," the trunks have been painted

white. To one side is a tiny enclosed secret garden while at the farthest end of the property there is a circle garden planted with vinca and *Pieris japonica*. More steps, bordered on one side by seven silver cube planters filled with Hosta *Fortunei* 'Minuteman,' chosen because their lavender flowers grow straight up and don't lean over, complete the walk around the house.

Linear and functional, this garden is full of spatial awareness, and it has a breathtaking simplicity. Plants, trees, stone, and gravel are the building blocks that Bergmann has used to make a cool, complex garden that is full of constantly changing vignettes and appears to be far larger than it actually is. In the words of a recent visitor, "The mixture of texture and geometry, the architecture of it all, took my breath away."

By the Sea

A seaside garden possesses its own special charms. Ruud Bergmans's garden is not directly on Long Island Sound, but it is just two miles inland on the edge of a tidal river. Water, marshland, and the sandbars visible at low tide are dominant features of this site's captivating natural landscape. A low bridge limits traffic to small boats, and except for the occasional crabber, Bergmans's garden is utterly private.

It was almost by chance that Ruud Bergmans and his wife, Ann Lane, put down roots in this part of Connecticut. In 1986, looking for a weekend house within two hours of New York City, they drew a circle and for no particular reason decided to begin their search in eastern Connecticut. Bergmans remembers telling the real estate agent, "Show us your three cheapest properties," and this small eighteenth-century house on the Black Hall River with less than two acres of land was the first they saw. It was so overgrown that no water was visible, but the agent assured them it was there, and they decided to purchase the property.

Bergmans never meant to have a garden. "At first," he recalls, "I only wanted to clean it up a little, but then I began to think it might be a good idea to have a bit of a plan." From there, he proceeded to do everything himself. As a child in Holland, he worked in his parents' garden, and although his childhood efforts had begun simply as a way to gain his father's attention, he discovered he enjoyed gardening and kept at it. This experience has served him well.

Today visitors enter the garden through a gate leading from a small parking area at the far right of the property and walk past an old schoolhouse that Bergmans has connected to the house with a simple pergola covered with Dutchman's pipe. To the left of the gate is a dense border of trees and shrubs planted in front of a stone wall that runs parallel to the road, blocking the sight and sound of traffic and hiding a deer fence. At one end a huge Norway spruce forms an impressive backdrop, lightened by a sweep of lacecap hydrangeas. Next come large mounds of boxwood softened by a mass of Japanese snowballs that start out chartreuse in early spring and slowly turn white. A towering evergreen *Chamaecyparis obtusa* 'Nana Pyramidalis' forms a canopy over the border. Next to it is another more formal but less used entrance gate and beyond this holly, a swath of leatherleaf viburnum, and more boxwood.

The windows of the living room overlook a rectangular rose garden, a bed that started out small and square but which Bergmans doubled in size several years later when his plan to install a pool at its far end was denied by the local planning board. This garden features many varieties of David Austin roses, including 'Gertrude Jekyll,' 'Tess of

the d'Urbervilles' 'The Mayflower,' 'The Prince,' and 'Tradescant,' commingled with caryopteris—a simple but effective combination.

Bergmans did finally obtain permission to build a small, square pool, and he sited it between the rose garden and the far end of the border that lines the road. Set into the lawn, the pool sits at the center of a predominantly white garden that Bergmans has softened with the chartreuses and pale yellows of alchemilla, potentilla, kirengeshoma, and most conspicious of all, a magnificent *Chamaecyparis obtusa* 'Crispii.'

It is at the back of the house, where the boundary between natural landscape and man-made garden blurs, that one becomes most conscious of the surrounding wetlands. The two borders that extend the entire length of the property are separated from each other by steps leading down to a dock. The border on the left is bathed all day in

sunlight and planted with a heady profusion of pink and red rugosa roses intermixed with lavender, buddleia, vitex, vernonia, and junipers. The border to the right of the dock is almost entirely in shade. Scotch pine, cedar, and swamp black cherries are interspersed with clethra, witchhazel, oakleaf and Annabelle hydrangeas, a smoke-bush, kirengeshoma, ligularia, and weeping hemlock. A large group of miscanthus helps ease the transition to the marshland beyond.

There is nothing pretentious or fussy about either the garden or its gardener, who admits that he never reads garden books cover to cover, preferring instead to "just dip into them," leaves out pots of hydrangeas to survive the winter—or not, and off-handedly pronounces the grass to be "terrible." And yet Bergmans's "bit of a plan" has become not only a haven for butterflies and birds, including the seagulls that circle overhead, but a beguiling garden that fits with unruffled ease into the larger seascape.

Exuberant Plantings

"A cottage garden with aspirations" is how Frederick Bland describes his plot of less than an acre that is home to somewhere between 1,400 and 1,500 plants. There are sixteen varieties of clematis, seventeen varieties of euphorbia, and nineteen kinds of heuchera. And if that were not enough, Bland has created a cross-referenced computerized index where each plant is listed by its Latin name, common name, source, and the date he acquired it. "Creating this list, which runs to more than twenty pages, was a lot of fun" but, he says, "keeping it up-to-date is a load of work."

What makes it even more astonishing is that this wonder gardener is also a practicing architect in New York and escapes to his garden only on weekends. In 1993 he and his wife purchased what he describes as "this broken-down little cottage, formerly a garage" on a plot of land that measured about fifty by three hundred feet. He was not in the least deterred by the size. "Coming from the city, it seemed big to me," he explains. "The only garden I had ever had was on a seventeen-by-thirty-foot Brooklyn roof."

From the outset, he had strong ideas about the kind of layout he wanted—a double border was part of his initial plan. Later on, he was able to purchase the house next door and its garden, which was wider and sunnier than his own. His neighbor, "a spectacularly fabulous person and a great intrinsic gardener," was then ninety-seven years old. They worked out an arrangement whereby he could take over the garden and she could stay in the house for the rest of her life. Her one stipulation was that Bland must never do anything to her pussy willow. Of course, it was sited exactly where he wanted to build a pool, so, with her permission, he carefully moved it, and it still thrives today. When she died four years later, in 2001, he renovated the house and added a conservatory. He also began to think about how to make the two gardens into one. Once he had put in a terrace and gravel garden as well as a large double border in the original space, he realized the eye needed a rest and created a diagonal grass meadow to cut across both spaces and offer a long view.

Today the long double border boasts an extraordinarily rich mix of perennials, grasses, shrubs, and small trees. Full of interesting and unusual juxtapositions, it takes its inspiration from the famous long border at Great Dixter, created by the English gardener Christopher Lloyd. Clematis 'Betty Corning' climbs through the yellow tips of *Chamaecyparis pisifera* 'Filafera Aurea,' behind a clump of salvia 'Van Houttei,' which has dark burgundy bracts. The salvia sits in front of a *Yucca filamentosa* 'Color Guard.' The purple leaves of *Rosa glauca* and the lavender flowers of *Thalictrum rochebruneanum* intertwine behind two *Berberis thunbergii* ('Aurea' and 'Rosy Glow') placed near blue oatgrass at the border's edge. By late August a pink Japanese anemone joins the party, as does bronze fennel, an uninvited but welcome guest. The border is anchored

throughout with a tall, dark green yew hedge and a number of boxwood cultivars. These are barely visible by late summer but do important work in the winter by providing a strong contrast to the grasses in the bed, which are never cut down before April Fools Day.

Bland's extensive knowledge of plants has been fostered by his long involvement with the Brooklyn Botanic Garden, where he is now chairman of the Board of Trustees. Wave Hill has also been an inspiration. "I am a collector at heart," he confesses. "I can't go to auctions or look at catalogs without getting weak in the knees and buying more than I should. On the other hand, being an architect, I have to work to make visual combinations that please me." With his plantsman's sensibilities and strong sense of design, he has made his small garden with big aspirations vibrant and sophisticated.

In the Southern Manner

Captain's Folly is a New England garden imbued with the spirit of Virginia, where its owner, Edward Lee Cave, was born and brought up. Gunston Hall, best known for its exquisitely carved interiors, Kenmore, George Washington's boyhood home in Fredericksburg, and Hammond Hall in Annapolis are the houses Cave remembers from his childhood, and red bricks, white columns, and boxwood remain close to his heart.

In 1981, Cave, who worked with Sotheby's, went to see a collection of American furniture in a house in a small Connecticut village half an hour north of Hartford, close to the Massachusetts border. Another reason for the visit was to gently explain to the owner that, given its obscure location, this would not be an easy house to sell. Although Cave had gone to school in New England and was familiar with the colonial American tradition, he had never been to this part of Connecticut before nor was he looking to buy a house. But he recounts, "From the moment I came down the drive, I knew immediately and without a doubt that I had to have this house." He bought it a week later for the full asking price.

He purchased what he describes as a modest New England farmhouse that had been added to over the years. At some point, a lean-to shed was attached to one side, and in the 1940s, a wing was added to give the house an attractive front courtyard. The property is reached by a long winding drive, once a road, that leads past an orchard and a very large barn, which is actually three separate barns joined together. Stone walls, dug three feet into the earth to better withstand the harsh winter temperatures, surround the grounds. Wanting to re-create an eighteenth-century colonial garden, the previous owners had made an herb garden out of six square beds in the front courtyard and a larger, fenced-in garden at the back of the house. The latter had patterned beds, intersected by a network of brick paths, and was filled with plants suitable for medicinal and household use, such as digitalis, pulmonaria, old-fashioned rugosa roses, bedstraw (once used for stuffing mattresses), lilacs, and peonies.

"Never allow hybrid tea roses in my garden" were the owner's parting words to Cave. For a year he "respected what was there and did nothing." Then he set about making his own imprint. First, to give the property more privacy, he closed in the side that was open to the fields by planting hemlocks, pine, and spruce. Next he installed an eight-foot fence around the perimeter of his land to keep out the deer. After making a careful survey of all the trees—there were some magnificent old maples on the property and a stand of venerable red pines—he added some specimen trees, including a copper beech, some Japanese maples, a clump of willows, and a Judas tree. He also planted a grove of white birches, his personal salute to Saint Petersburg. White roses, trumpet vine, climbing hydrangeas, and clematis were trained to grow up the trunks of the

apple trees in the orchard—an idea resulting from a visit to Sissinghurst. Virginia blue-bells, his father's favorite flower, were planted in the main garden, and primulas and daffodils in other parts of the property.

Cave's parents were enthusiastic gardeners, and he remembers as a child waking up at dawn and going to work with his mother in her garden. "She was a very good gardener, and thanks to her I've learned not to make any terrible mistakes." He placed curved boxwood hedging around the six square beds in the front of the house, and by planting horseradish, fennel, basil, dill, and peppers, he has created what he calls "a culinary garden with good aesthetics." In the main fenced-in garden, his additions

include geraniums, salvia, monarda, miniature sedum, many more roses (but no hybrid teas), standard hydrangeas, southernwood *(Artemisia abrotanum)*, tree peonies, cleome, lamb's ears, iris, and black-eyed Susans.

An oak tree that shaded the terrace at the back of the house was destroyed some years ago by a hurricane, and in its place, Cave made a rock garden, planting bergenia, sedum, thyme, and different species of fern. "I tried to think about alpines, but they're just too small," he says. A mass of yellow daylilies, all from a single, divided clump, covers the hillside beyond, and pots of agapanthus, a plant he has loved since childhood, adorn the terrace.

Asked about his gardening philosophy, Cave will only say, "If I'm in a nursery and see something wonderful, I now get it right away. I've learned you may never see it again." He thinks of himself as something of a taskmaster, admitting, "I hate weeds and have even been accused of vacuuming my woods." But he has achieved so much more than a weed-free garden. The authentic but rigid colonial American garden he purchased has become less strictly orchestrated, more relaxed, and filled with a joyful exuberance. Cave describes what he has done as an attempt to make the garden "a little less controlled, a little less serious." There may be no white columns, but his garden radiates Southern charm. A visit to this garden reveals Cave's intimate relationship with each and every one of his plants, and many of these denizens of Virginia are perfectly content, even so far north.

Hillside Terrain

"I had no idea of what I was getting into," Eva Ching recalls as she scrambles down a pathway of stone steps that traverses the precipitous descent from her house to Lake Wononskopomuc. Sweeps of ferns, white astilbe, columbine, and hosta gently spill out of crevices between huge rock ledges. The planting has been kept very simple with nothing fidgety or over-complicated and each twist and turn of the slope reveals a different vista to delight the eye. There is the constant sound of a cascading waterfall, and although the setting is dramatic, the mood is tranquil and contemplative—a wooded paradise that is worlds removed from what Ching found ten years ago when she and her husband purchased their house in Lakeville. All that existed then was a frighteningly sheer slope covered with a jungle of overgrown bushes and trees and intersected by a narrow track held in place by rotting railroad tires.

It was daunting, especially for someone without any previous gardening experience. However, Ching, who is an interior designer, decided the only thing to do was to deal with it as she would a professional assignment, beginning with research. First, she signed on for a trip to see English gardens with her friend and garden designer Renny Reynolds. "Tell me what this is," she would ask him endlessly, as they visited garden after garden. Armed with a notebook, she spent all her time writing down the names of plants she liked, only to realize later that 80 percent of them needed sun and were inappropriate for her shady wilderness.

Reynolds persuaded her to excavate the waterfall that previous owners had constructed. Through Judy Murphy, a local garden designer and owner of a nearby nursery, she met Nick DeAngelis, known as "the rock man." He gave her several different proposals, and she settled on a fairly simple plan to reopen the waterfall and make a series of stone steps leading down from the house to the lake. But as she watched DeAngelis begin to move huge stones and boulders into place and reveal the natural rock face, she realized he was a master craftsman, whose skill could not only create a path but define a much needed structure for her rocky hillside. Having persuaded her husband they should increase their budget, she gave DeAngelis the go-ahead to carve out several planting areas, instructing him to create "more drama." It is a decision she has never regretted.

Ching relied on Murphy for technical advice on what to plant, but the process was always collaborative. When they decided to plant a grove of silver birches near the water, Ching wanted five trees but this seemed too many. Murphy proposed four, but in Chinese the word for "four" rhymes with the word for death, so they finally settled on three. When Murphy proposed planting a swath of ribbon grass nearby, Ching suggested adding ferns and came up with the idea of setting the trees in gravel.

As the garden began to take shape, Ching grew surer about what she was doing and more aware of the freedom that comes from the discipline of using a limited color palette. Foliage and texture took on new importance as rock outcroppings were planted with sweeps of maidenhair fern, Japanese painted fern, bird's nest juniper, liriope, rhododendron underplanted with astoiboides, and different varieties of hosta. Creeping geranium and pachysandra (a plant she feels has been unfairly maligned) now cover much of the plunging vertical overhang of the rocky hillside. The garden has taken on a life of its own with clumps of native ginger and dwarf euphorbia appearing from nowhere and moss, once scarcely in evidence, now blanketing many of the rocks.

Innisfree (a nearby Chinese landscape garden, created more than fifty years ago by landscape designer Walter Beck and open to the public) has been a source of inspiration. Its rugged topography frames a sequence of self-contained pictures that visitors can walk into as they choose and enjoy without distraction. These may be an enframed meadow, a lotus pool, or a single rock. Each picture or "cup" garden, the term Beck liked to use, draws attention to something rare or beautiful, and sometimes several cup gardens may be contained within a larger one. In this type of garden, natural elements such as water, terraces, rock outcroppings, and plants are used not only to define space but also to establish tension and motion.

At first, this concept made little sense to Ching, but gradually she began to grasp its meaning and she now experiences her own garden as a series of vignettes. She admits that in the beginning she was too caught up with the planting and the weeding and too focused on the final result to appreciate or to "see" the value of what she was doing.

Today, she finds what satisfies her most is the actual making of the garden. She is generous in crediting everyone who has worked on it, seeing herself as the orchestrator and knowing the key to success is finding the best people and giving them real latitude. Although she would be too modest to admit it, what she and those who work with her are doing is taking the terrain that nature has provided and shaping it into a work of art.

In the French Style

High clipped hedges, ornamental allées, topiaries and bosques, parterres laid out in the squares, circles, quincunxes, and rectangles of traditional formal Renaissance patterns: these are the hallmarks of a classical French garden. It is an aesthetic based not on natural forms but on symmetry and order, a style of gardening where flowers seem only an afterthought.

It is not what you would think of trying to create in the Connecticut woods, unless, of course, you are French, as Robert Couturier is, and this was the kind of garden you loved from childhood. When he and his partner, Jeffrey Morgan, purchased a sixteen-acre tract of land in northwest Connecticut overlooking North Spectacle Lake in 1999, Couturier, an interior designer who works in both the United States and Europe, designed a house that consists of a series of interconnected white clapboard pavilions with tall brick chimneys. Facing the lake, and with a steep hillside rising up behind it, the house has the unmistakable feel of a small, elegant French chateau. Such a house requires a French garden, and this is exactly what Couturier has created.

He first asked garden designer Miranda Brooks to come up with an overall garden plan. She proposed an allée of pleached hornbeams to be placed on axis with the rear of the house, a grouping of birch trees on either side of the allée, and two rectangular grass beds framed with two parallel lines of boxwood hedging. She also laid out a route for a long driveway that would begin at the road and wind through the woods to reach the house. Today it passes between an American colonial–style cottage and an eighteenth-century barn serving as gatehouses—a tribute perhaps to Morgan's American heritage or possibly to announce that Couturier has set down his French roots in Yankee soil. Descending the hill to the far right of the house, the drive passes a steep wooded slope banked with ferns, giving a few tantalizing glimpses of the garden before ending in a court paved in Belgian block and walled on the far side by three tall pleached hornbeams. From here visitors proceed on foot, past four square white planters, each containing a tall, rectangular mound of boxwood, to a formal courtyard in front of the house, from which there are magnificent views of the lake beyond.

Naturally, Couturier wanted a green garden. "Flowers only look good for such a short time," he laments. "Mon Dieu, in this part of the world, we can have heavy rain and storms till late May!" Like many Europeans, he still cannot quite believe the toughness of winter in Connecticut and recalls with horror one January storm when snow turned to freezing rain and sixty-three trees were lost. With a touch of Gallic optimism, he concedes that "this was not all bad, as it opened up the woods and got rid of some unwanted, scraggly trees."

67

In France a garden is planned to be seen primarily from the house, and every window should offer a view of it. In 2006, with this in mind, Couturier and Morgan asked Clive Lodge, a local garden designer, to adapt the original plan and also to extend the garden. Lodge's solution was to come up with what he lightheartedly calls "a mini Versailles." He replaced the birch tree groves on either side of the hornbeam allée with two formal parterres. Designed to be seen from the main living room of the house, which is on the upper floor of the central pavilion, each parterre is enclosed by a beech "wall" and contains an intricate series of swirling beds edged with boxwood. The paths are grass, and for the most part the beds contain no flowers, though a circular bed is planted with lady's mantle and at its center is an urn filled with 'Snowstorm' bacopa and dracena. A gravel path runs the length of the house and separates the allée and green parterre from the beds directly in front of the house. Lodge is also responsible for a long allée of *Viburnum x burkwoodii* leading to a high circle of yews that enclose an antique millstone, on which stands a large rare 1930s ceramic vase found by Couturier and Morgan in nearby Kent.

69

Two recent additions to the garden are a pin oak walk that runs through the woods and a lilac allée that leads from the yew circle to the road. Couturier recalls how as a child he loved the Comtesse de Ségur's *Old French Fairy Tales* and, having never forgotten the forest of lilacs in which Blondine gets lost, had always wanted to have lilacs in his garden. These lilacs give him particular pleasure, and they confirm how, with wit and finesse, he has created an unmistakably French garden in the hills of Connecticut.

73

Elegant Perfection

The spare geometry of Oscar and Annette de la Renta's mostly green garden is all about structure and architecture. She loves the discipline and drama of a precisely cut line. He focuses his attention more on the plantings and decorative elements. Their collaboration has resulted in a garden in which high yew hedges enclose a succession of simple garden rooms, three giant wedding-cake yew topiaries add drama to the vista of a magnificent double allée of pear trees, and the natural beauty of native birches, oaks, and sugar maples contrasts with the rigorous geometry of clipped boxwood and conical yews.

Many years ago, when de la Renta invited Russell Page, the great British landscape artist, to visit his newly purchased Connecticut farm and give him some advice, he was told in no uncertain terms that panoramic views and gardens do not mix. Standing on the terrace that stretched the width of the rear of the house, Page agreed that the view of open hillside and distant woods was indeed extraordinary, but then pronounced that this was no place to have a garden, since a garden is a room and rooms need walls, not views.

Page advised framing and enhancing the view but making a garden on lower, more protected ground to the far left of the house, where there was a barn. Although not the advice he had wanted or expected, de la Renta took it seriously. Today there is no garden at the rear of the house, only a long flagstone terrace (both the house and the terrace have been considerably extended) where large pots of agapanthus and boxwood are all that separate the house from its glorious view.

The main garden, tucked away from the house and reached by a short walk, has no connection to the house or to the open view. It is entered through a simple gate set between two high dry stone walls, and it encompasses a series of intimate garden rooms by high walls of clipped yew. The first of the rooms is a square formal garden laid out with boxwood-edged beds intersected by brick paths. It contains pots of herbs, four standard viburnums, a mass planting of perovskia under one of the long yew walls, and a neoclassical stone urn surrounded by a circle of boxwood in the center. An archway leads to a smaller room that used to be a rose garden, but after losing many of his favorite hybrid teas year after year to the intense winter cold, de la Renta replaced them with perennials. Gardens change over time, and the perennials have now given way to a more formal garden that is mostly green, except for the climbing roses that grow up four wooden Chatsworth blue tuteurs. Another room enclosing the swimming pool is planted with mounded boxwood of varying sizes interspersed with hydrangeas and junipers. Further on is an exquisitely simple enclosure with a fishpond in the middle and two rows of pleached lindens underplanted with boxwood on either side.

Beyond these enclosed gardens is a majestic double allée of *Pyrus calleryana* 'Redspire.'
It is the garden's most dramatic feature, but de la Renta says, "Had I known better,
I would never have done it with pears but used lindens or another tree with longer
life. After thirty years, pears start to crack, and I am beginning to have problems."
On the far side, a magnificent mixed shrub and perennial border more than 350 feet
long stretches the full length of the allée, and the three gigantic wedding-cake yew
topiaries rise up nearby. At the far end of the allée is a statue of Diana, goddess of the
hunt. She is holding a deer whose antlers are broken because, as de la Renta explains,
"Like most of the statuary in the garden, it came from my wife's former garden in

Katonah, where it was placed at the end of a long rectangular swimming pool and got damaged because her children used it as a diving board when she wouldn't install a more conventional one."

De la Renta insists his wife is the better gardener and has the more experienced eye. He credits her with reining in his inclination toward exuberant color and readily admits that they disagree often on garden matters. Currently in contention are four large honey-colored stone urns set on square pedestals that he purchased two years ago and placed in a line in front of a long yew hedge. She wants them to be moved, her rationale being that they look too much like Newport, which, she says, "Of course I love, but this *is* Connecticut." One has the feeling she will prevail. "I choose my battles" is her husband's diplomatic response.

He is already thinking of what comes next, and would like to level off part of the hillside at the rear of the house to better experience the depth of the view and to use the space to introduce a large "piece of water," such as a rectangular pond. He admits with a smile that serious negotiation with his wife about this plan has not yet begun. All he is willing to say at this juncture is "Annette hasn't as yet said no."

Almost Wild

Christina and Woodson Duncan live in a contemporary house that is one of three on a private drive. Although they have a little over four acres, most of their land is not around their house but on a steeply banked hill directly across the road. When they acquired the property in 2001, the Duncans had already decided they were not interested in having a traditional garden with formal beds and a lawn to mow. Instead, they wanted the year-round beauty of a wildflower meadow.

To see a meadow in bloom, its sweeps of color full of movement as it changes with every play of light and shadow, is to experience nature at its most alluring. But, random and natural though such a meadow looks, there is nothing haphazard about its creation. Just ask Larry Weaner, a professional landscape designer based in Pennsylvania who has planted more than one hundred meadows. He says that in the 1980s, when he first began, there was not much interest. Today, however, as understanding of climate change increases and interest in sustainable gardening gathers pace, his knowledge and skills are in constant demand. When gardening conversation turns to meadows, his name frequently comes up, so it is not surprising that when the Duncans decided they wanted a meadow, they sought his help.

When planting a meadow, Weaner uses only native plants and grasses, which for him means those that thrive in a particular soil and are most adaptive to a specific location. He generally uses seed mixes interspersed with some plants. Before a meadow can be planted, however, the ground must be cleared and all the weeds killed. Often this is done with commercial herbicides, but for the Duncans' meadow Weaner used a vinegar-based organic herbicide followed by an application of sulfur. The design challenge here was to plan the height of the plants so as to create a seamless view of the meadow and the woodlands beyond from the house while obscuring the view of the road and the next-door neighbor's lawn.

A perennial meadow is not a thing of beauty in its first year, since during that first growing season it needs to be mowed frequently to prevent any flowering. All that can be seen at this stage is a shallow layer of oat grass, which Weaner uses as a nursing crop—so called because it protects the seedlings from being choked by aggressive weeds. Patience is essential, and even in its second year there is still not much to see. But then black-eyed Susans and coreopsis began emerging as part of a first wave of flowers in the Duncans' meadow, followed by slower-growing perennials, including baptisia, eryngium, eupatorium, liatris, penstemon, monarda, asters, and lupins.

Today the meadow, a rarity among the manicured lawns in this predominantly suburban community, presents an ever-changing display of subtle colors and blooms. Yellows and

88

pinks predominate in the summer, turning to more of a lavender and white palette by fall, while seedpods and grasses rigid with frost add sparkle to the winter landscape.

The Duncans are delighted not only with their low-maintenance, drought-tolerant garden, which is mown only once a year in the spring, but also with the amazing number of birds and butterflies attracted to it. Song sparrows, kestrels, red-tailed and Cooper's hawks, goldfinches, bluebirds, and wrens are all regular visitors, as are hummingbirds and dragonflies. During early summer, the fields are filled with "a symphony" of crickets, and on summer nights the air is rich with fireflies. Their meadow has indeed become their garden, its texture, movement, and color a source of endless interest and pleasure throughout the year.

Perfectly Simple

Nancy McCabe is a garden designer whose trademark is a lack of pretension. She is a perfectionist who values restraint and dislikes gardens that seem "overdone." Having a singular eye for quality and detail and a reputation for speaking her mind, she is not one for compromise, and if clients disagree with her approach, she is the first to tell them to seek out another designer. McCabe lives in Falls Village, and many of the gardens she has designed over the years are nearby. One of her favorites is a small garden that belongs to Isabel Fowlkes and her husband, Winston.

The Fowlkeses live in a small barn converted to a house that sits in a garden of less than an acre, on property that had belonged to Winston's family. Twenty years ago, when Fowlkes asked McCabe to give her some ideas and to help with the design of the garden, she wasn't starting with a blank slate. Shrubbery screened the house from the dirt road, and a low stone wall, which her husband had built himself, connected the house with another barn that serves as a garage. A large rhododendron was already growing up the wall of the barn, and its abundant deep purple-pink blooms and extraordinary height of more than twenty feet still make it the most spectacular feature of the garden.

McCabe proposed underplanting the oak and laurel in the shrubbery with white rhododendrons and white azaleas, both to make the hedging into a spectacular spring showpiece and to further shield the house from the road. McCabe suggested adding bearded iris to the peonies and other perennials planted in the long border that runs the length of the lawn on the far side of the stone wall. She also introduced large groupings of boxwood, dramatically clipped into undulating, abstract shapes, at intervals among the perennials. They add structure and interest to the garden in winter and are a variation on the more formal boxwood buttresses that McCabe had planted in her own perennial border, which Fowlkes had greatly admired.

A terrace on the far side of the house was substantially changed and enlarged when the Fowlkeses added a new dining room to their house. A low perimeter stone wall was expanded and rebuilt, and small beds were placed among the bluestone pavers to give the terrace the feel of a small French potager. The beds have been planted with herbs, including sorrel, sage, tarragon, and basil, and with tender annuals such as verbena, cosmos, white zinnias, and heliotrope. Pots filled with lilies, acidanthera, roses, buddleia, and brugmansia are scattered around the terrace. Two tree-form wisterias add height, their twisted trunks offering a perfect contrast to the straight lines of the terrace. The Chippendale-style chairs, copied from a Lutyens design and bought in England, are perfectly in keeping with the spirit of this outdoor room.

95

97

To this day, Fowlkes remembers McCabe's first visit to the garden. Much to the owners' horror, one of her first suggestions was that they remove their newly installed Scott swimming pool, which had been set into the sloping lawn so that it could be seen from the terrace. Since this was not going to happen, McCabe persuaded them to make it more in keeping with the landscape by removing the decorative boulders and rocks that had been so carefully placed around it, redoing the coping to make it as simple as possible, and insisting that the plastic skimmer caps be replaced with ones made of bronze.

Fowlkes admits, "When Nancy was so outspoken in her dislike of the pool, I was at first taken aback, but then I realized that it was precisely because of such judgments that I had asked her to work with me on my garden." Today they are the greatest of friends, and these many years later the success of this collaboration is apparent. All the elements and different parts of the garden interact harmoniously, the structure evident but never overwhelming. It is a garden whose romance is delightful but whose simplicity is never less than immensely appealing.

Benevolent Supervision

Phlox, peonies, lupins, feverfew, salvia, clethra, iris, sedum, lamium, clematis, and campanula have the run of Nancy Grant's garden. She dotes on her old-fashioned perennials and, like an indulgent mother, lets them climb, creep, weave, and spread at will. Delphiniums, "those pesky creatures" are harder to grow, but she wouldn't dream of giving up on any of them. Roses are another passion; she has mostly David Austin and older varieties such as Ispahan (a damask rose that grows wild on the hills of Iran) and New Dawn. "No hybrid teas—they just don't work for me," she declares with the kind of knowledge that comes only from years of dealing with tough Connecticut winters. Her beds are edged with nepeta and ladies mantle that she has propagated herself, and almost all the large freestanding balls of boxwood come from cuttings taken from two small pots of Korean boxwood she purchased in the 1970s when she first began work on her garden.

The Grants purchased their 1730s clapboard house in 1969. During restoration, it burned to the ground. Undeterred, they set about building an exact replica of the original. For a garden similar to what would have existed in the eighteenth century, the Grants consulted a professor of garden design and restoration at the University of Connecticut. He proposed a layout with four quadrant beds and provided a plant list appropriate for an historic American garden. While their children were growing up, the Grants concentrated on vegetables and fruit, but once the children left home, their focus shifted to flowers. In came the peonies and there are now more than 100 of them growing in a single bed. Beginning in late May, the fragrance of their pastel feathery petals and luscious heavy headed blooms are, in fact, the crowning triumph of this gentle cottage garden.

Over the years, the Grants have created a landscape that is perfectly in keeping with the house and its setting. Here is a garden where the benefits of age and maturity are evident for all to see. "People think we're a little crazy to carry on year after year with this garden but we love it and want to live and garden this way as long as we can," says Nancy Grant. There's not a hint of hesitation in her voice.

A Garden of Art

Agnes Gund loves to see sculpture out of doors, especially big, monumental pieces. "It is enormously interesting," she says, "to be able to look at a piece from a distance, something simply not possible when looking at sculpture in a contained indoor space." While other garden owners worry about the placement of their beds, Gund's foremost concern was to site each piece correctly. "It's critical, as I want a work to have some coherence with the scenery and not be overwhelmed, for instance, by a large tree."

Close to her farmhouse is *Fruit Loop*, a large steel work by Mark De Suvero, installed in 2004, that her grandchildren love to climb all over. "And they do," she admits. Nearby is a cedar wood sculpture made by Ursula von Rydingsvard that resembles a rough-hewn bowl. Rising up in front of an old red barn is *Curve XII* by Ellsworth Kelly, a piece she bought many years ago and had always wanted to put outside on account of its size. Spanning an entire hillside and most dramatic of all is *Iron Mountain Run*, a sculpture she commissioned from Richard Serra in 2002. Before making the piece, Serra, "spent a long time walking over the land and decided he wanted to create a work that would move down a hill." This site-specific piece is about the visual relationships that emerge from the unorthodox siting of seven steel plates (each one is fifteen feet high). A driveway follows the contours of the meadow allowing the work to be seen from many angles and distances. Serra's installation is a bold and unforgettable use of garden space.

109

A Woodland Refuge

"I can say it's beautiful," says Anne Harrison, speaking of her woodland garden, "but that's because I didn't make it. My job has been to preserve it." What she modestly calls preservation represents more than a decade of work enhancing and extending the natural gifts of this garden. The house was built in 1929, constructed of local stone in a Gothic style and dramatically sited on a series of steep rocky outcroppings that fall sharply away to a lake below. A steep slate roof and tall stone chimney add to the feeling of its being a French chateau tucked deep in the woods. The vertical drop is punctuated by several levels, connected by a series of walls, terraces, and steps, which create a variety of lookout points and vistas. This sophisticated hardscaping was done with great craftsmanship and is thought to date to the time the house was built.

Harrison and her husband, Bill, purchased the property in 1997, and since then they have enlarged the rear terrace and added greatly to the plantings on the terraced levels. Balls of boxwood have been placed on both sides of a winding, stepped pathway to provide more definition, and lichen has been encouraged to spread over the treads of the wide, formal outdoor steps that descend in a straight line from the center of the terrace to the expanse of lawn. Beyond this is a boating lake, which is fed by a nearby creek and contains three small islands. A small gazebo has been placed on a further hill, and a pool is tucked away at one side of the lawn.

With the help of designer Tim Paterson, who, according to Harrison, "keeps us on the straight and narrow," the couple has worked hard to reveal more of the huge rock outcroppings on their property. Paterson believes that the strength of the natural landscape is what makes this garden special, and he has encouraged the Harrisons to enhance and dramatize what already existed. The undergrowth has been cleared to reveal more of the rock, carpets of moss have been gently cultivated to spread beneath the ash, maples, oaks, poplars, and willow trees that enclose the garden, and walking trails have been created throughout.

Azaleas laid out in drifts are combined with redbud and Florida dogwood trees. Forget-me-nots, columbines, and foxgloves have been encouraged to spread and colonize. A stream was made by channeling water from a small pond down a rocky outcropping, and an existing ravine was widened and made into another stream, using stones from the property. Ostrich, cinnamon, and royal ferns line its banks, and flag iris and sweet woodruff are planted nearby. In spring, winter aconite, snowdrops, scilla, and chionodoxa flower in quick succession. Next come carpets of bluebells; by summer the hydrangeas are the stars of the garden. There's a magical quality to this woodland garden with its sweeping shafts of wildflowers scattered beneath mature trees, a place so much in harmony with its natural setting.

INGE HECKEL 🌿 LAKEVILLE

"A Host of Golden Daffodils"

"Fluttering and dancing in the breeze," these Wordsworthian daffodils in Inge Heckel's garden are a glorious reminder that winter is finally over and spring has arrived, always a cause for celebration. Thanks to a previous owner who planted thousands of bulbs every year from 1930s until the early 1980s, Heckel's chief responsibility is to fill in any bare patches and mow the field twice a year. This low-maintenance garden is a breathtaking April sight and passers by blink, stop, and gaze mesmerized at this ravishing sweep of more than fifty thousand daffodils stretching as far as the eye can see in front of Heckel's picture-perfect 1790s saltbox.

Modern Masterpiece

Perched in a hilltop meadow with magnificent views of the surrounding Litchfield hills, Jack Hyland and Larry Wente's house and garden fit so seamlessly into the landscape that they seem to have always been there. However, it was only in 2002 that Hyland and Wente purchased forty-one acres of land on this farthest edge of Connecticut's northwest corner (the state border runs across their property) and began work on the treeless, overexposed site—scarcely ideal conditions for a garden.

Wente is an architect specializing in sustainable construction, and he designed their house, a modernist structure that features a tower rising like a silo above a group of barn-like shapes, to conserve energy, water, and materials. It has a metal roof, radiant heating, solar panels, and a passive ventilation system. The garden is similarly environmentally friendly. Runoff from the front-door overhang flows into two large planters placed on either side of the entrance, which hold a combination of canna lilies, helichrysum, and deep-purple potato vine. Rainwater is also collected from the main roofs and stored in two huge underground cisterns behind the garage. It is used to irrigate the garden, and if the system runs low it is automatically replenished from a local spring.

For both practical and aesthetic reasons, the house was built using a four-foot grid, and this structure extends into the garden, determining the shape and dimensions of the beds and underscoring the strong relationship between house and garden. The house has eight doors that open invitingly into different parts of the garden and yield breathtaking views. "Our primary goal," says Wente, "was to make the inside and the outside feel part of the same experience." He was in charge of the overall plan and shape of the garden while Hyland, an experienced plantsman, took the lead in making the horticultural decisions. Wente was "tired of long, wide perennial borders," and Hyland was intrigued by the idea of using primarily grasses and native plants as a way to connect the garden to the surrounding open fields.

The main area of the garden, only about a quarter of an acre, is a long and narrow rectangular space that extends the footprint of the house. It is divided into a series of narrow beds alternating with straight grass paths that lead to a swimming pool. At the far end, the pool equipment is hidden in two sheds, one of which doubles as a small sculpture studio. Two huge compost boxes sit next to rows of cobalt-colored solar panels that are accentuated rather than disguised, as is usually the case. Farther on, adjacent to a small, contained orchard, is a meditative garden featuring a forty-foot long rill, inspired by the Alhambra and fed by water trickling from a bamboo pipe. Its bluestone coping is bordered with a luxuriant mass of variegated hosta interplanted with spider-wort. Decorative elements are limited to four antique stone fence posts once used to tether cattle, and an Indonesian bench.

126

The beds close to the house are planted with a variety of grasses, some limited to a single type of grass and others containing grasses mixed with alliums, nepeta, cosmos, and verbena. Texture rather than color is emphasized, and the boldness of the plant groupings, many of them reaching to a height of five feet, provides a dramatic contrast to the formality of the overall grid design. The loose waving and blowing of the grasses gives the garden a luminous quality. A long cedar pergola covered with wisteria lines up with the chief axis of the house, not only functioning as a covered walkway to the pool but also providing strong verticality in contrast with the strict horizontality of the grid layout. Elsewhere height is achieved with conical upright junipers, trellising, high hedging, and two lines of oversize wrought-iron plant tuteurs, each playfully holding a reflective globe.

Hyland and Wente dealt with the initial lack of trees by planting a copse of maples beyond the garden proper but in an area clearly visible from the house, where a swath of spruce and white pine also acts as a windbreak. Between the trees and the garden

they planted an annual wildflower meadow, which Hyland reseeds every year. While the main garden is rectilinear, Hyland and Wente cleverly opted for a different strategy for the main approach to the house. The curving drive turns back on itself, and a stone path going to the front door cuts across the upper part of the drive and delivers the first direct view of the house's silo, which rises dramatically like a Tuscan bell tower. The path is bordered on one side by an orchard of mature crab apples that lends a sense of age. Purple-flowering verbena bonariensis and the grass *Deschampsia cespitosa* 'Schottland' are planted in a square bed to its right, and beyond this is a smaller bed with three native shad trees and goldenrod, which by late August comes alive in a blaze of gold.

"Taming the meadow" is how Hyland describes the process of creating this garden, but this is far too modest a description for the strong architectural character and canny logic of this breathtaking garden.

All Grown Up

Roxana Laughlin has known her garden since childhood. It belonged to her parents'
neighbors, a couple with no children who were enthusiastic gardeners. After they died
in the 1950s, Laughlin's mother bought the property and eventually it passed to her
daughter, who has lived there since 2001 with her husband, Ledlie.

"Even though I was familiar with the garden, I wanted to do something new that
would be my own contribution," says Laughlin about her decision to renovate rather
than restore the garden. This meant respecting its historic structure but redigging
and re-creating the beds. Bounded by old stone walls, the garden occupies about three-
quarters of an acre. The focal point had been a large perennial border that wrapped
around three sides of a central lawn to the left of the house, but when Laughlin took
over, the borders had long since gone to seed and were thick with weeds. Although
she had a general sense of what might work, she turned to her friend Tiziana Hardy,
who lives nearby in Massachusetts and takes on design projects from time to time.

Wanting to break up the large, square lawn, Hardy took some of the large flat stones
that at one time had formed the foundation of the house, placed them in an asymmet-
rical pattern on a bed of gravel in the center of the space, and then surrounded them
with low-growing 'Winter Gem' and 'Green Velvet' boxwood. Over time, the boxwood
has grown into undulating mounds with subtle variations of color and texture. What
Hardy refers to as "a dry stone river," a feature found in many Japanese gardens, miti-
gates the straight edges of the lawn and has introduced a new aesthetic into this
otherwise traditional garden.

135

To ensure a steady succession of blooms for the outside borders, Hardy devised a
planting scheme that salvaged the magnolias and delphiniums and uses a combination of perennials mixed with shrubs such as buddleia, spirea, and hydrangea. Spring
bulbs flower in April and May, while June brings peonies and delphiniums, followed
by nepeta, lavender, and lilies. In midsummer, color is provided by phlox, perovskia,
and clematis.

Mindful of landscape architect Russell Page's injunction to leave enough flat land
around a house so that anyone stepping out the door has an immediate sense of space,
Laughlin decided to add a little earth to the steep rear ridge of the property. As a
result, the drop-off has been pushed farther back from the house. Still, the grass on
the steepest part of the lawn was difficult to mow, so Laughlin planted two sweeps of
ornamental grasses along this section of the ridge. They offer a pleasing contrast to
the more formal look of the planted beds, and maintain a textured presence throughout the fall. A former peony bed on the far side of the ridge has become another

impressively long mixed border, glimpses of which can be seen from the unpaved road leading to the house. From her childhood visits, Laughlin remembered a linked series of small ponds that allowed water to tumble down a rocky hill to a larger pond put in by the former owners. Over time this water path had silted over, and uncovering it to create a water garden became another reclamation venture.

The month of June, when the peonies are blooming, is Laughlin's favorite time of year. But it is every year in April, with the arrival of spring, that more recent memories mingle with old, and she knows that this garden, remembered from her childhood but skillfully reinterpreted, has truly become her own.

Gardening with Panache

Lee Link's property is perched almost at the top of a very steep hill with breathtaking views. Her garden has been in the making since 1980 and is very much an extension of the house, which she and her husband, Fritz, have transformed over the years from a rather severe wooden A-frame into a far more interesting and eclectic piece of architecture. The garden surrounds the house and can be seen from every room, thereby blurring the distinction between indoors and outdoors. This is particularly so in the screened porch and the conservatory dining room the Links added, where that distinction all but disappears.

A long, low stone wall serves as a boundary between the house and the distant rolling hills. After an unsuccessful attempt to make a garden on the intervening slope, Link brought in a bulldozer and terraced the space, putting in a narrow, stone-edged fishpond and planting a clipped yew hedge along the stone wall to further emphasize the separation of the garden from the natural landscape beyond. Next came a flower bed close to the house and later a large perennial border in front of the screened porch, the straight lines of these beds contrasting with the contours of the open countryside. Two square terraces, one off the screened porch, the other in front of the conservatory dining room, which serves as the main entrance to the house, underscore the close relationship between house and garden, as does a wooden pergola, covered in vines and wisteria, which connects the main house to the guest house. Link cheerfully pronounces the wisteria to be a big mistake since it needs to be cut back every ten days. A line of four large buddleia bushes flanks the courtyard entrance and parking area, and a row of silver birch trees screens the front of the guest house, which also faces this courtyard.

One of the charms of this garden is that there is very little that is predictable about Link's choice of what to grow. She has a penchant for bold architectural plants, a weakness for succulents, and likes nothing better than to mix vegetables with annuals. In the border beside the house she changes the planting every season and has an uncanny talent for coming up with unlikely combinations—lettuces are paired with nasturtiums, pansies with perilla, and snapdragons with leeks.

Link likes "mass planting" and has one bed, below the screened porch, filled entirely with Russian sage. A stunning woodland garden on the steep rock ledge behind the house offers long sweeps of hosta. This part of the garden got started by accident—the result of a trip to a bankrupt nursery that offered Link all their hosta for only two dollars apiece. It was too good a deal to refuse, but only when she got home did she realize she now had to do something with them. And that typifies the way this garden has evolved. No grand plan, nothing on paper, just an ability to respond creatively to an unexpected opportunity, adapt an idea she has seen elsewhere (her row of silver

141

birches was inspired by a lecture given by garden writer Helen Dillon), and, if something isn't quite right, the patience to tinker with it until she is satisfied.

Two years ago, Link made the controversial decision to remove the main perennial border. Her rationale was extremely practical: "It took a lot of work, cost a lot of money, and I decided I wanted less garden to take care of." But since it was an astonishingly beautiful border filled with shrubs, tall perennials, and annuals in a bold mix of yellow, chartreuse, purple, and plum, the reaction of her friends to this flagrant act of "bordercide" ranged from horror and incredulity to wide-eyed admiration. Her mind made up, Link divided the space into three square beds, edged them with Belgian block, and placed a multi stemmed *Cornus kousa* within each square. The middle bed is underplanted with Japanese painted ferns and the two outer beds with a creeping potentilla, which hasn't yet measured up to her standards and will probably be replaced with heuchera. It was a radical change, but one that she does not for a moment regret.

145

Come winter, Link moves her operational base to the greenhouse, where she continues to enjoy herself, however cold and forbidding the weather outside. Her original idea was to have "something quite modest—a place to grow more plants from seed—but once I got started somehow it kept getting bigger." What she finally ended up with is a bespoke greenhouse that reveals a meticulous attention to detail. Spacious and functional, it is divided into three separate temperature zones. "I adore being in the greenhouse any time of the year but particularly in winter, and I have such a good time there that I can't imagine life in the country without it," she says. Begonias, rare geraniums, tree ferns, papyrus, delicate euphorbias and huge bulbous aloes all rub shoulders in this indoor paradise. In addition to an ever-expanding seed-growing industry, there are rows of orchids all being gently coaxed back into bloom, a collection of camellias, lots of bulbs—not just narcissus but tulips, iris, muscari, hyacinths, and galanthus.

Over the years, Link has assembled a marvelously unorthodox collection of urns, eclectic antique ornaments, lanterns and, her latest addition, chunks of slag glass she found on eBay. These objects, along with huge pots filled with agaves and other succulents, are judiciously placed throughout the garden, adding a gentle touch of humor to the boldness of the plantings. Link has a way of making it all seem quite effortless, a lot of fun, and a place where she can indulge herself in doing what she likes most of all: "just puttering around my plants."

Many Colors, Many Moods

After passing through a narrow, white arched gateway to the right of Lynden Miller's house, visitors turn a corner and come face-to-face with this garden's most dramatic feature—a high, curving hedge of clipped yew (*Taxus x media* 'Hicksii') that extends almost two hundred feet in length.

When Miller and her husband, Leigh, purchased their white clapboard house more than thirty years ago, there was no garden—only a rather too visible swimming pool. Miller, an urban horticulturalist, put in the hedge to block the view of the pool and to create an enclosed garden area near the house. "In order to shape the property and the view beyond, making the hedge curved felt right, and still does today," she explains. The yews have also formed a dark evergreen backdrop for a colorful border of shrubs, perennials, bulbs, and annuals, all carefully chosen to ensure interest throughout the year. Here, Miller fearlessly juxtaposes bold colors, setting off blues (nepeta, baptisia, salvias, hibiscus, and perovskia) and purples (barberry, smokebush, thalictrum, and heuchera) against cimicifuga, artemisia, drifts of phlox, and ornamental grasses.

Three white arched gateways in the hedge interrupt its sweep and provide access to what lies beyond. The central opening offers the vista of a meadow and reveals a mown grass path leading to a simple white pergola and curved bench. The arch on the right leads to a crab apple allée underplanted with daylilies and daffodils, while that on the left leads to the pool, now well concealed. To the right of the allée, Miller has established an informal nursery garden, where newer plants can get their footing and she can experiment. To the left of the house is a woodland garden and beyond the nursery is her newest project, a small water garden with a pond fed by a recirculating stream.

Miller has a particular love of hydrangeas. Not content to grow only those varieties hardy in zone 5, she craves the big pink and blue bushy-flowered *Hydrangea macrophylla* that flourish in zone 6 and up. Her favorites include 'Endless Summer,' 'Merritt's Supreme,' 'Madame Emile Mouillere,' 'Glowing Embers,' and, of course, 'Nikko Blue,' and her gardener, Dan Garren, has devised an ingenious regimen that allows these varieties of hydrangea to thrive. Each fall, he digs them up and stacks them on their sides, covers the pile with pine needles and leaves, and tops it all with a plastic tarp. When spring arrives, they are released from their enforced dormancy to be replanted in borders or repotted and placed throughout the garden. The effect is startling and original—strong pinks and blues interspersed throughout the border to give a prolonged summer of glorious mophead blooms. It is a bold move—but, then, this is a bold garden full of delightful surprises.

Studiously Understated

"How did you ever find a place like this?" is a question often asked by visitors when they see the magnificent views, rolling green fields, and stone walls surrounding the house that Nancy Newcomb and her husband, John Hargraves, finished building in 1991. The answer is simple: this idyllic natural-looking landscape was not found but made with care and determination over a period of more than twenty years.

When Newcomb and Hargraves purchased a forty-acre parcel of land in 1986 (later acquiring an additional twenty acres) the land was so thick with brush and second-growth woodland that there was no view and no open space except for one field full of unsightly tree stumps covered with giant suckers. In spite of this, Newcomb was convinced there must be a view and indeed there was. Clearing the land and removing the boulders, some of them as large as cars, was a formidable task but, as the earth was gradually uncovered, a network of crumbling dry stone walls appeared, conclusive proof that this had been open farmland in the eighteenth and nineteenth centuries.

Lester Collins, a well-known landscape architect and trustee of Innisfree, the famous Chinese-inspired garden in Millbrook, New York, was recommended to Newcomb by her architect. He helped her decide which walls to keep and which to eliminate. A local mason took on the task of rebuilding those that had tumbled down, and today these walls not only define the space but are one of the most beautiful features of this intelligently crafted landscape.

A long drive leads from the road past an orchard of crab apples to the house, which sits in a spare gravel courtyard, its entrance framed by two small pavilions. Putting in an orchard was Collins's idea. He was also responsible for planting a stand of *Kousa* trees to the right of the drive and for suggesting the grouping of small pine trees around the huge lone pine that survived the initial clearing. Boxwood and inkberry bushes are planted close to the house, but it is the glorious vista of meadows and stone walls framed by a line of woods beyond that capture the visitor's attention.

Newcomb recalls Collins, who died in 1993, with great fondness. "He never imposed, only suggested," she says. For the past ten years, she has relied on landscape designer Douglas Reed to help her refine the spareness of her unadorned landscape garden, finding his sensibility remarkably similar to Collins's. He has altered the placement of the shrubs around the house, moved some of the hawthorn trees that were blocking the view from the terrace at the rear of the house, and is now working with Newcomb to thin out the trees in the orchard and to make a cedar boardwalk path in a wetlands area bordering a pond.

157

To an untrained eye, Newcomb's garden might appear to be an expanse of grazing farmland—its open fields a legacy from another century. But the genius of this spare landscape garden lies in the way it has been allowed to settle into the prevailing spirit of place. Sensitivity and understatement make this a garden where less is truly more.

A Consummate Collector

Nearly ninety years old, Nick Nickou is without a doubt Connecticut's preeminent plant collector. He is legendary, and his garden is a place of pilgrimage for serious plantspeople, who come from far and wide to observe, study, and marvel at the amazing variety of his collection.

Although he had wanted to be a farmer or a horticulturist, Nickou was sent to medical school while serving in the United States Army during World War II. When he was first discharged, he practiced medicine in Ohio, but he later moved with his wife and seven children to Branford, where he has been living in the same house ever since. Although working as a general practitioner, he used all his spare time to assemble what is now acknowledged to be one of the most interesting plant collections in the United States. Until quite recently, he would make at least two expeditions a year, not to bring back seeds or plants but to observe, record, photograph, and learn about rare and unusual plants. His travels have taken him to Greece, Australia, Hawaii, Turkey, the Himalayas, Iceland, Greenland, Spain, Russia, South Africa, the Alps, and China.

Nickou thinks of himself as more botanist than gardener, and shrubs are his greatest interest. He has the largest collection of rhododendron (more than one hundred specimens) in New England and an extraordinary number of woody plants, including species of *Enkianthus*, *Magnolia*, *Acer*, and *Daphne*, as well as numerous alpines. He is also an acknowledged fern "fiend." The three-acre garden now resembles a giant horticultural museum. As its curator-in-chief, Nickou likes nothing better than to take visitors on tours, pointing out unusual specimens, such as his huge clump of *Arisaema ringens*, and his prized *Magnolia macrophylla*, now eighty feet tall with impressive two-foot-long leaves and enormous creamy white flowers, that he planted about forty years ago within view of his dining room. Nickou delights, too, in fooling unsuspecting visitors. He might, for example, refer to his "dwarf" ginkgo tree—a specimen that is only five feet tall after thirty years in his garden—and deliberately fail to mention that there is no such thing as a dwarf variety but an ordinary ginkgo that he cuts back almost to the ground every spring.

Nickou's garden is remarkable not just for its horticultural curiosities but also for its array of tender shrubs and trees. The garden sits solidly in zone 6, but an eight-foot *Camellia japonica* 'Kumasaka' seems to have no problems with the winters in Connecticut, where temperatures can drop to more than ten degrees below zero. Planted against a wall of the house are *Crinum x powellii* (Cape lilies), not usually grown out of doors in the United States except in zones 10 and 11. And an oversize *Aucuba japonica* 'Variegata,' supposedly not hardy any farther north than zone 7, is clearly content in this garden.

One of Nickou's prize possessions is *Trochodendron aralioides*, a wheel tree virtually unknown to most American gardeners and, according to the experts, only possible to grow in zone 8.

Remarkably, Nickou does not wrap or cover any of his plants in winter. Instead, he relies on his meticulous research on a plant's soil requirements and sun or shade preferences. "It all has to do with the siting," he explains. His garden is on a steep hill that drops down to a lake, and the cold air drains down the hill, which itself gives the plants a lot of wind protection and helps them avoid winter burn. Drainage is another important consideration, and he puts his tenderest plants in raised beds filled with organic matter mixed with peat.

Today Nickou is ably assisted by his second wife, Carol, also a keen gardener. His first wife died in 1992, and he and Carol met in 1997 at a plant meeting. As she explains, "I came to visit and never left." And why would anyone want to leave this plantsman's paradise?

A Glory of Roses

Constance Spry, Bobbie James, William Baffin, and Sara Van Fleet are only some of those who grace Melissa Orme's garden. But not at cocktail parties or afternoon tea—they are her favorite roses whom she treats as honored guests. They bloom for her in glorious profusion throughout the month of June and into July and never, she swears, cause her the slightest trouble.

It was almost twenty years ago that Orme and her husband, Paul, bought their farmhouse—parts of which date back to the eighteenth century—and Orme started preparing the ground for planting. Before they settled in Ridgefield, the Ormes had lived in many parts of the world and visited many gardens. But it was the celebrated rose garden at Kiftsgate Court in England and the formal and elegant Villa Gamberaia near Florence that Orme says "have been the inspiration for everything I've done in my own garden."

The property behind the house slopes steeply, and when Orme, herself a garden designer, first set about planning the main sections of her garden, she carved out a level area halfway down the hill. Orme's roses are approached from the rear of the house, via a path as charming as the garden itself. The path passes through an allée of ten crabapple trees (*Malus* 'Sugar Tyme') planted at right angles to the slope, which leads to a dramatic entranceway flanked by giant balls of variegated ivy and pots of standard *Rosa* 'Baby Blanket.' Inside the garden proper, gravel paths and boxwood edge four-square, symmetrical outside beds planted with roses interspersed with delicate perennials, including platycodon, monarda, lady's mantle, nepeta, lilies, and amsonia. Each bed has at its center a beautiful standard lilac tree of astonishing breadth grafted to a remarkably slender trunk. The trees are as striking in winter as they are in full bloom in the late spring and offer a deliciously formal counterpoint to the fragrant clusters of roses that grow around them.

Indeed, Orme's entire garden can be seen as a study in contrasts: circles within squares, formality amid profusion. At the heart of her four-square layout is a circular bed bordered by boxwood and planted with a simple combination of lime thyme, variegated strawberries, and curly chives. But an old urn set in the middle of the bed and planted with iris, silvery sedum, and blue petunias provides a distinct focal point. In spring, tulips push up in the center bed while forget-me-nots and black violets, self-seeded over the years, romp happily onto the gravel paths.

Once spring is over, the garden is primarily about the roses, which are Orme's particular passion. She generally prefers the fragrant old-fashioned varieties that bloom heavily for a month to the modern so-called repeater varieties that, in her experience,

never quite live up to their promise. She buys her roses from a nursery in Pickering, Ontario, on the theory that if they can survive the winters in that climate, they can surely manage the rigors of Connecticut. Having a practical outlook, she believes that "if it doesn't do well, too bad—it goes."

A tunneled arbor entwined with a lavish display of *Rosa* 'John Cabot' leads from the rose garden and down a few steps to a small, elegant knot garden bounded by tall, columnar apple trees. Beyond this are a stream and a woodland garden, and off to one side is Orme's vegetable garden. A long peony walk winds back toward the house by way of a shrub garden filled with rugosa roses, spirea, lilacs, and hydrangeas. Nothing seems contrived or overdone in Orme's creation: just a little Tuscan magic crossed with English charm and thoughtfully transposed to Connecticut.

Rare Shrubs and Trees

The garden surrounding the early-twentieth-century stuccoed house Michael Rosenthal bought in 1981 featured an uninterrupted view of Long Island Sound. It stood at the highest spot on Killam's Point, a narrow spit of land in Branford that reaches out into the Sound, and it also adjoined a wildlife preserve. However, the semiformal garden planted by the previous owners had been neglected—the terraced levels were almost completely obscured, and the roses had grown wild. Brush choked the wooded area around the house and covered the rock ledges on which the house was built.

One of Rosenthal's most vivid memories of those early days is the magnifying glass and tweezers he kept in his office so he could pull out thorns on Monday mornings. "I had no idea," he says, "of what I was getting into," but he sought advice from good sources. Lester Collins, a landscape architect who also taught at Harvard, was a minimalist and he recommended ripping out everything and starting over. This was not what Rosenthal wanted to hear, but he credits Collins with teaching him to see and think about the garden as a whole. The next expert Rosenthal consulted was unable to take on the job but offered one very practical suggestion: "Never work on more than ten square feet at a time. This way, if things go wrong, you will make only a small mess." Rosenthal appreciated the logic of this admonition.

Unable to find someone to do the work, Rosenthal decided to tackle the Herculean task on his own, and he has been doing it ever since. First he defined the steep pathway from the house to the lawn—later enlarged so his children could play softball—by edging it with a mass planting of *Juniperus procumbens* 'Nana.' Next he removed large amounts of poison ivy from the rock ledges nearest to the house and interspersed the lichen-covered rock with sweeps of hakone grass. His first serious plant purchase was a weeping blue cedar (*Cedrus atlantica* 'Glauca Pendula'), which he trained to grow up one side of the house and now stretches majestically along the full length of the wall.

Following the "do a bit at a time" rule, Rosenthal cut away more overgrowth each year and greatly simplified what remained of the formal terraced garden by removing a vegetable area and cutting back on the peonies. The roses stayed, however, and the garden now contains over ninety varieties, including floribunda, hybrid teas, shrubs, and climbers, ranging from rugosa roses to 'David Austin.' Rosenthal belongs to the school of tough love: "I don't feed my plants—just good soil and water are what they get to live on. It's a regime that seems to work for them and for me."

As time went on, trees and shrubs came to overshadow his interest in perennials, and today his garden boasts an extraordinary collection of unusual types.

He can proudly show visitors many rare Daphnes, more than sixteen varieties of hydrangeas, thirty varieties of maples, several magnolias, many larches, six different dogwoods, and eleven varieties of viburnum. There are six varieties of dogwood trees, a Franklin tree (*Franklinia alatamaha*), two Stewartias, a Katsura tree (*Cercidiphyllum japonicum* 'Heronswood Globe') whose flowers emit a cotton-candy fragrance in late fall, two *Heptacodium miconoides*, and more than forty varieties of hosta.

Rosenthal's garden presents striking contrasts at almost every turn. Several lookout points high on rock ledges open up dramatic sea vistas, the woodland landscape possesses an intimate charm, the roses put on a lavish display, and rare specimen trees and shrubs are everywhere.

Rosenthal, who has traveled the path from total ignorance to being an accomplished gardener, explains that one of the ways he learned so fast and so well was by "going as often as possible to Twombly Nursery in nearby Monroe and spending two to three hours just wandering around," something he still loves to do. He also describes himself as having a Zen mentality when it comes to gardening. "Yes," he says, "I did everything myself, but then, too, I really had nothing to do with it."

Nature on a Grand Scale

189

The dramatic backdrop to John and Julia Scott's multilevel garden is a magnificent waterfall, its rim seen here, framed by giant petasites. After plunging more than twenty feet, it weaves a meandering path through rocks and boulders, making the presence of water evident both visually and audibly in every part of this steep hillside garden. In summer the waterfall is deceptively gentle; in winter, its cascading action is often dramatically frozen into huge icy stalactites. But it is in spring that it unleashes its power with unrepentant, almost terrifying abandon.

By English Rules

Gillian Steel honed her gardening skills while living in a house with a garden in London in the early 1990s. She attended courses at the Chelsea Physic Garden, visited any number of English gardens, and still clearly remembers being astonished by Vita Sackville-West's garden at Sissinghurst. These experiences stood her in good stead when she and her husband moved back to the States in 1994 and bought a house in Greenwich.

She counts it as great luck that a friend introduced her to Tim Paterson, an English garden designer who lives and works in and around Westchester County. Together they set to work to create an English-style garden, the most unusual feature of which is the terrace running the full length of the back of the house. Although the choice of container plants placed there varies a little from year to year, Paterson and Steel tend toward cool pastels. Blue is the predominant color, with salvias, lantana, and plumbago much in evidence. Over time, the terrace has evolved into three distinct rooms, with seating on the far left, a dining area in the middle space, and an area, accessed through an opening in a tall yew hedge and adjacent to the kitchen, where Steel has an outdoor fireplace and pots of herbs.

Paterson transformed a circular driveway in front of the house into a formal courtyard and framed the space with boxwood sentinels that provide winter interest. Mindful of the English adage that a garden does not belong at the front of a house, but wanting to provide a tapestry of interest, he came up with a remarkably subtle planting scheme. In early spring, blue and white crocuses emerge from strips of grass around the courtyard. Next comes scilla, followed by the delicate blooms of Yoshino cherry trees, which have been underplanted with daffodils. White tulips tucked in behind the boxwood begin to flower by early May, proceeded by a dramatic display of huge white gladiator alliums and, then, the flowers of 'President Grevy' and 'Madame Lemoine' lilacs. Finally, a profusion of 'Annabelle' hydrangeas burst forth in this garden that is all style and no pretension.

191

Italian Overtones

Step into Michael Trapp's garden and enter a world where tangled flowers spill over ancient statuary and plinths, balustrades, and columns line winding cobblestone paths. Although less than three-quarters of an acre and only a stone's throw from the main street of West Cornwall, this is no ordinary village garden. The effect is infinitely more Tuscany than Connecticut.

Trapp is an antiques dealer specializing in large-scale statuary, furniture of elegant decrepitude, cracked but ravishing china, faded textiles, and all kinds of unexpected architectural objects. He is also a designer both indoors and out, and his garden is not just an extension of his house and store but a reflection of his skill in recycling what-ever comes his way. The kind of transformation he likes to engineer is not so much a look or style but the result of a philosophy that permeates the way he lives and works. "I like things to look old, wild, and enchanting, as if they've been here forever," he says.

The main entrance to the garden is through two shutters salvaged from a nineteenth-century church and turned into doors. Flanked by four wooden Ionic columns, they open up to a cobblestone terrace where silver-leafed santolina, myrtle, rosemary, and Marguerite daisies grow in terra-cotta pots set on stone balusters. Beyond the terrace, what was once an unprepossessing garage has been transformed into an exquisite gar-den house that now serves as an office for Trapp's design business.

The dominant feature of the upper garden is a long reflecting pool complete with resident goldfish and water lilies. Water drips and gurgles from a nineteenth-century neoclassical Italian fountain, and the pool is bordered on both sides by six tower-ing junipers, now so tall that pruning requires elaborate scaffolding. At the far end, another cobblestone terrace offers a sweeping view of the Housatonic River. Six raised flowerbeds of different shapes, intersected by narrow cobblestone paths, fit like pieces of a jigsaw puzzle around the pool. They are edged with boxwood, and the planting is intentionally simple—monarda, alliums, white lilies (*Camassia cusickii* and *Camassia leichtlinii* 'Blue Danube'), foxgloves, nepeta, hollyhocks, Joe Pye weed, thalictrum, and angelica gigas. Some of the beds have trellises and colonnades planted with pink wisteria, 'Betty Prior' roses, autumn clematis, and purple leaf grapes.

Dropping thirty-five feet below the upper garden, what was once a small and shady strip of grass has been transformed into a wonderfully original garden reached by a series of stone steps cut into the precipitous hillside. Trapp has used the steep slope to astonishing effect. He has built a small grotto into the hillside, which serves as an unexpected and original pool house for the lap pool it adjoins. The floor is made of antique marble slabs brought from Antwerp, and shards of ancient coral, found

by Trapp many years ago in Florida, are stashed in an alcove, adding to the sense of exotica. Three sides of the pool house are built into the hill, making it a cool spot even on the hottest days of summer. Turn-of-the-century French doors give onto a terrace paved with seventeenth-century French limestone that borders the pool, which rises above ground on three sides, making it appear to float in space. Apart from wisteria climbing over the grotto, there is hardly a flower in sight. Instead one finds the green foliage of hosta, giant petasites, myrtle, and boxwood. "The last thing I needed was more maintenance," Trapp explains.

What's surprising is that the inspiration for Trapp's magical garden is all practical ingenuity. There's also almost no grass in this garden because he dislikes having to mow. At the far end of the lower garden a humble tool shed, which Trapp has made into a freestanding library to house his collection of chiefs' hats from Malawi, is carefully positioned to hide the pool equipment.

Local stone has been used to make walls and steps throughout the garden, and eighty-eight tons of cobblestones, once part of an abandoned road in eastern Connecticut, have been painstakingly laid out by hand to make the terraces and paths. The various parts of Trapp's garden seem like stage sets with the garden furnishings, all marvelously eclectic, making up the scenery. They include Palladian windows salvaged from the Rhode Island statehouse, massive Cretan oil jars, iron finials from Ohio, a Florentine lion's head, a monumental urn from a garden in Minneapolis, and stone balustrades found somewhere in the Midwest.

Some people restore; Michael Trapp reinvents. A tour de force of illusionist art, his garden brims with imagination, its scale and extended perspective astonishing for such a small space. With all the strong lines, beauty, and theater of a classic Italian garden, Trapp has created a place of true enchantment.

Tradition Renewed

Surprisingly, it is not known who originally laid out the garden plan for Rosemary Weaver's house, but it was clearly someone who understood how to integrate a garden into its setting. The majestic trees, rolling driveway, spare courtyard, high hemlock hedging, and walled-in garden are all perfectly in keeping with the neoclassical architecture of the elegant stone house, which was designed by James C. Mackenzie Jr. in 1939 for George Brett Jr., president of Macmillan Publishing.

Weaver's late husband bought the property in 1968. He was an enthusiastic gardener, more knowledgeable about trees than plants, but as he got older and was able to do less, the garden began to show signs of neglect. Fortunately, in 2000 Wendy Weaver Chaix, his daughter from his first marriage, enrolled in the landscape design and horticulture program at the New York Botanical Garden. Realizing what a learning experience her father's garden could be, and wanting to have a laboratory to test her newly acquired skills, she proposed to her father that she get involved. He was delighted to have her help.

Chaix's first task was to identify what was there. Her father was never one to throw anything away and loved the task of dividing his plants. As a result the garden was rife with astilbe and Siberian iris, and its beds desperately needed organizing. To give them more structure, she simplified the planting and enlarged groupings of single species. Her stepmother favors pastels, so Chaix removed most of the reds and oranges, planting lady's mantle, aster, salvia, and lambs' ears in their place. Since this was not her own garden, she learned, however, to be diplomat as well as plantswoman: her father never failed to notice when she made a change and would always insist on knowing what had happened to any plant she removed.

207

When her stepmother requested a white garden, Chaix transformed what had been a semicircular rose garden into one for her. Surrounded by a high, curving yew hedge, it is filled today with a gentle mix of white allium, potentilla, phlox, and nicotiana.

Chaix's father died in 2003, and since then Chaix has continued rejuvenating the formal borders of the walled garden. She has also simplified the plantings around the swimming pool, thinned the trees in the woodland area that borders the drive, and replaced part of the hemlock hedging, one of the most distinctive features of the garden. Chaix is modest about her role as caretaker, but the renewed vigor of this quietly elegant traditional garden is the result of her watchful eye and benevolent supervision. And for Mrs. Weaver, the garden continues to serve as a meaningful reminder of her husband.

All About Style

There's so much to love about Bunny Williams's garden: the bold scale of the perennial borders; the ornamental flair of an enclosed parterre potager; the late summer opulence of the large kitchen garden; the quiet charms of a meandering woodland garden; and a romantic conservatory filled with tender scented plants. All are part of what makes her garden such a special experience.

Williams's assured sense of style is everywhere apparent. She approaches a garden with the same sensibility as she would an interior space and has created a series of rooms, each with its own character. A stroll through her garden reveals an astute balance between the formal and informal. Much of what gives it such a distinctive personality is the number of unexpected elements she has incorporated into these rooms. An early-nineteenth-century picket fence, salvaged from Maine and discovered at the Farmington antiques fair now encloses the kitchen garden and a Victorian iron compost bin, piled high with clippings, is both useful and decorative. "I think of them as my props," Williams explains. "I use them to lend my garden architecture."

She has also paid a great deal of attention to the "places in between"—the pathways, steps, doorways, and entrances that form the connections and links between the garden spaces. A decorative urn flanked by tall arborvitae posing as cypress and set at the top of thyme-covered steps becomes a destination. She calls it her "Italian moment." An eight-hooped pergola covered with autumn clematis turns a gravel pathway into a charming semi-enclosed protected walkway, while an antique faux-bois cement table and chairs placed in a corner of the woodland garden offer the possibility of a leisurely picnic. Three huge topiaried yews underplanted with a sea of vinca lend elegance and definition to a covered loggia that runs along one side of the Federal-era house while an octagonal wire aviary with flanking pavilions provides a touch of chinoiserie and houses white fantail pigeons and some very exotic chickens.

213

The parterre garden, which adjoins the conservatory extending off the barn, was inspired by Rosemary Verey's kitchen garden, but over the years it has become a little more formal. Bordered by a simple gray fence, it is composed of four beds intersected by brick paths, edged with Victorian rope tiles, and divided by boxwood that forms its own crisscross pattern. Each year this garden takes on a new color scheme: first it is planted with masses of tulips and bulbs and later in the season with annuals. One year, they are all white, the next blue, and so on. Two standard dwarf Korean lilac trees in the middle of the largest beds provide vertical interest while a double metal archway and a rusticated locust pergola running the full length of one side are key structural elements in the overall effect.

One of Williams's more recent pleasures is the woodland garden, which she began working on a few years ago. First, she cut a path through the woods on the outer edge of the property, inserted steps where needed, and constructed a pond and waterfall at a natural dip of the land. Then planting began in earnest with hundreds of spring bulbs—fritillaria, daffodils, scilla, and crocus—together with primulas, ferns, tipularias, epimediums, and viburnum. Still a work in progress, the woods have been tamed and are now a significant area of her garden.

Her current project was inspired by a recent visit to look at gardens designed by Jacques Wirtz in Belgium. It is a long yew hedge Williams has planted around a large expanse of lawn that lies between the sunken garden and the parterre. Its top edge is purposefully cut to give an undulating ribbonlike effect, and when it reaches maturity, it will transform a somewhat forgotten space into a high-walled room.

No good garden ever stands still, and Williams is always thinking about what to do next. She describes herself as a person "tempted by possibilities," but this characteristic is tempered by an ability to constantly refine what's already there. The result is a stunning garden with an exuberance and vitality that reflects both its owner's marvelous imagination and good old-fashioned sense.

Bending the Rules

Peter Wooster never intended for his garden to be looked at from outside its low gray picket fence. Instead, to experience this unconventional garden properly, a visitor needs to enter through the gate that always stands open, put aside any preconceptions, and suspend disbelief. This garden has been more than twenty years in the making, and if Wooster is to be believed, he had no idea that what started out as a small, pleasant plot would turn into something so tantalizing and unpredictable.

The layout of this rectangular garden is straightforward enough. Six identical oversized, oblong beds are separated by one central grass aisle and a grid of grass paths. The edges of the paths used to be meticulously straightened each year, but they have become so narrow that Wooster no longer lets them be trimmed. The result is a charmingly slight but distinct undulation in their lines. The garden beds can be viewed from every side of these paths, and there are no vistas, no eye-catching views, no destinations other than along one central aisle of grass that cuts across the middle of the garden. Here there is a group of Adirondack chairs, a circular Victorian bed planted each year with a mix of annuals and tender perennials, and a shingled Ehrick Rossiter parasol, found by Wooster in a nearby garden, which stands guard over a table of nonhardy potted treasures.

If the layout is simple, the look of the garden is anything but. By midsummer, a visitor is immersed in dense layers of vertical plants that emerge from a carpet of ground covers and low perennials. Wooster loves to play with scale and height and has no compunction about placing tall plants such as plume poppies, castor beans, elephant ear, *Nicotiana sylvestris*, thalictrum, and even a banana tree at the outer edges of his beds. Hollyhocks, amaranthus, verbascum, and ornamental grasses vie for attention, and none of the usual conventions of placement seem to have been applied. The planting is at once complex and simple, and the effect of this glorious overload is lush, immediate, and dramatic. Wooster has also created a bold collision of colors using oranges, hot pinks, reds, and bright yellows: there are no restrictions on those sharp hues that most gardeners nervously keep at bay. No gradual transitions here, no careful sweeps of color—just plant upon plant upon plant.

Contributing to the garden's impact is that it has seemingly magic growing powers: the plants are enormous, annuals reseed, and even many of the tenderest species thrive. The secret? The previous owner kept cows and threw all his manure onto his vegetable plot, which became the site for the present garden.

Wooster is a plant collector par excellence, and he is aided and abetted by his gardener, Rob Girard, who seems able to keep tabs on every specialty nursery in America and who nurtures and coddles tender perennials, succulents, and exotic annuals in the nearby

227

greenhouse that serves as the critical power center of the garden. Wooster is reputed to have once said he never met a plant he didn't like, and this passion for plants is the hallmark of his garden. Bulbs, annuals, perennials, exotics, and vines happily cohabit, and this astonishing abundance of horticultural diversity never misses a beat.

231